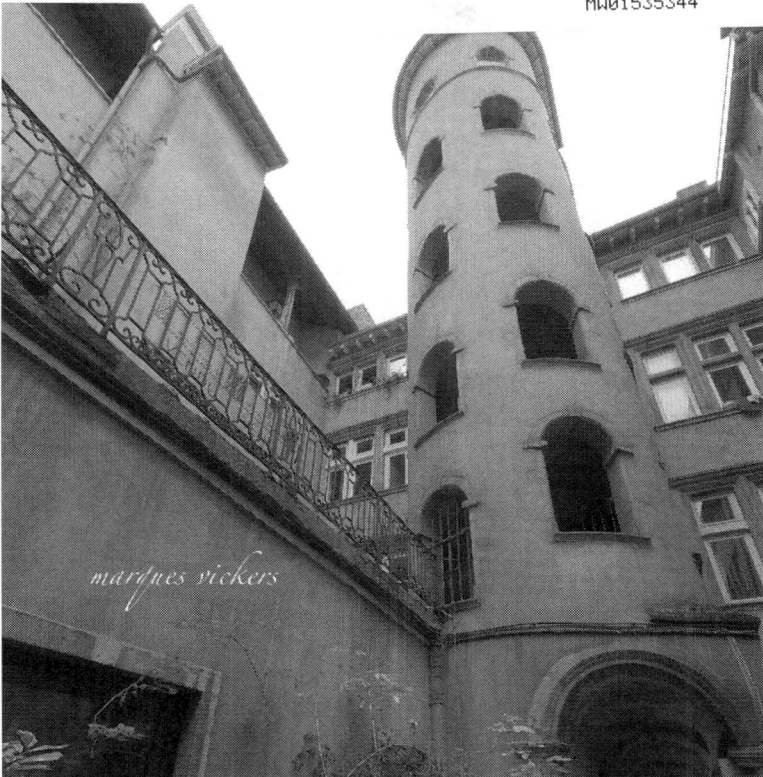

marques vickers

LYON, FRANCE PASSAGEWAYS:
ROMAN AQUEDUCT OF GIER, TRABOULES AND BRIDGES

Lyon, France Passageways:

Roman Aqueduct of Gier, Traboules and Bridges

By Marques Vickers

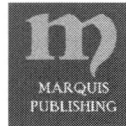

MARQUIS PUBLISHING
BAINBRIDGE ISLAND, WASHINGTON

@2023 Marques Vickers

All rights reserved. Copyright under Berne Copyright Convention, Universal Copyright Convention, and Pan-American Copyright Convention. No part of this book may be reproduced, stored in a retrieval system, or transmitted in any form, or by any means, electronic, mechanical, photocopying, recording, or otherwise, without prior permission of the author or publisher.

Version 1.1

Published by Marquis Publishing
Bainbridge Island, Washington

Vickers, Marques, 1957

Lyon, France Passageways:
Roman Aqueduct of Gier, Traboules and Bridges

Dedicated to My Daughters Charline and Caroline.
Thanks For The Photographic and Transportation Assistance.

SOURCES: ThisIsLyon.fr, VisiterLyon.com, HistoryHit.com, TheCollector.com, Wikipedia.org, Aqueduc-Romain-du-Gier.fr, *Parcours Saint-Etienne et Sa Metropole* by Saint Etienne Office of Tourism *L'Aqueduc Romain du Gier* by Mayor's Office of Chaponost Sentier de L'Aqueduc Romain du Gier and OffbeatFrance.com.

INSIDER SERIES BOOKS.com

TABLE OF CONTENTS

PREFACE

This edition intimately portrays Lyon's famous Traboules, the Roman Aqueduct of Gier, renowned passageways within the city and bridges that line both the Saone and Rhone Rivers.

Traboules are clandestine passageways winding through buildings and courtyards. Each passage is unique and often features buildings with pastel colors, confounding curves, arches, vaulted ceilings and spiral staircases. Each traboule radiates mystery and intrigue within the shadows. Many boast a Renaissance era heritage with some dating back to reportedly the 4th century.

An estimated 400 traboules exist within Lyon with approximately 40 identified by a small blue lion emblem and open to public access. Inhabitants of the Roman colony of Lugdunum established residences on the banks of the Saone River due to the lack of fresh running water. The lower *Vieux Ville* (old city) settlement was established at the foot of Fourviere Hill. The traboules were designed to permit expedient access for residents to the river.

Silk production was once the major industry within Lyon. The silk workers numbering approximately 25,000 were called *Canuts*. They became a prominent presence within the neighborhoods during the early 19th century. They employed the passageways to carry their heavy textile workloads from their Croix-Rousse district workshops to textile merchants at the foot of the hill.

The Roman **Gier Aqueduct** was constructed during the 1st and 2nd Centuries presumably during Emperor Hadrian's reign. His substantial legacy included construction projects throughout the Roman Empire and a wall named after him located in northern Britain.

The aqueduct was originally sourced from the Gier River on Mount Pilat, the largest peak of three located in a range outside of St. Etienne, to the southwest of Lyon. Legend attributes that the body of Roman Governor Pontius Pilate was buried there. The aqueduct transported fresh water 53 miles until it reached its summit and termination location upon Fourviere Hill within the 5th arrondissement of Lyon.

The aqueduct was constructed of stone, brick and fastened by volcanic cement called Pozzolana. The design traveled inhospitable terrain employing vaulted masonry arches, a complex piping system and Siphon bridges that forced the flow uphill. Much of the structure remains today. The most picturesque ruins are photographed in this edition and located in the communes of Mornant, Chaponost and Saint-Foy-Les Lyon.

Lyon is a pedestrian-friendly city burdened by steep and flinty inclines. The inlaid stone pathways and staircases reveal stunning architecture, commercial offerings and ancient historic sites. Many of the routes were developed amidst some of Lyon's most turbulent and influential historical events.

Eighteen bridges are photographed crossing the Saone and Rhone Rivers to complete the passageway profile. The book's overall view, background descriptions and sweeping panorama offer a stunning composite of France's third largest city. Lyon contains a distinctive mixture of ancient and contemporary influences with a major urban center and periphery.

THE AQUEDUCT OF GIER

The Roman Senate ordered the creation of a settlement in 43 BC for refugees of war in the conflict with the Allobroges. The relocated population had been expelled from Vienne, an important trading center during the Roman Empire located approximately 22 miles away from the present day Lyon. The group initially encamped at the confluence of the Saone and Rhone rivers, located on the southern periphery of the contemporary city. The foundation of the initial settlement was constructed upon the highlands of Fourviere Hill. The colony became known as Lugdunum translated into the Gaullist language as *Desired Mountain*.

Lugdunum's strategic location became a desirable starting point for essential roads within the region. The settlement would evolve into the capital of the province, Galla Lugdunensis. Two future Roman emperors, Claudius and Caracalla were born in the city, the sons of government officials. Preserved remains of the ancient Theatre of Fourviere and the Amphitheatre of the Three Gauls testify to the formerly advanced development.

Burgundians fleeing the nomadic Hun tribes from the Caucasus resettled in the region during 437 AD. Six years later, the Romans established the Kingdom of the Burgundians claiming Lugdunum as its capitol. During the dark ages and the emergence of feudalism, the territory became absorbed into the Kingdom of Arles and later Holy Roman Empire. Burgundy would evolve into Europe's wealthiest and most dominant power by the 15th century before the abrupt death of leader Duke Charles the Bold. The kingdom was dismantled and absorbed into France by King Louis XI.

Four aqueducts fed fresh water into the Lugdunum settlement. The longest and best preserved is the Aqueduct of the Gier that sourced its waters from the Gier River, a right bank tributary of the much larger Rhone River. The Gier flows in a northeastern direction through the present French Loire and Rhone departments. The Gier valley would later become heavy industrialized with coal and iron mines and factories.

The Gier Aqueduct was constructed during the 1st and 2nd Centuries AD. In 1887, a stone with an inscription mentioning Roman Emperor Hadrian's name was discovered near Chaponost. This discovery has become a basis for dating the origins of the construction. Hadrian served as emperor for nineteen years from 117 to 136 AD. His substantial legacy included construction projects throughout the Roman Empire and a wall named after him located in northern Britain.

The aqueduct was originally sourced on Mount Pilat, the largest peak of three located in a range outside of St. Etienne, to the southwest of Lyon. Legend attributes that the body of Roman Governor Pontius Pilate was buried there. The commune of Saint-Chamond in the Loire department of the Auvergne-Rhone-Alps is the credited commencement point for the aqueduct water flow.

The settlement developed on both sides of the Gier River. Throughout the 53 miles that the aqueduct follows, the routing traces the bends and serpentine conditions of the topography. Stretches would be literally designed around villages to take advantage of the straightest and flattest landscape. Roman engineers took advantage of gravity whenever possible to forward the water flow. The pace of the flow became critical.

The aqueduct sloped downwards from lakes and springs regulating the speed. If the water moved too quickly, the effect would wear down the stones. If the water moved too slowly, it would become stagnate and impotable. Much of their design involved redirecting water to sloping lands even if it required a diversion miles away from its ultimate destination. Layered arched bridges filled deep valleys and water flowed atop in the open air.

One of the most ingenious innovations involved the utilizing the *penstock technique*. Floodgates were established to regulate the water flow. Pressurized siphons enabled water to travel uphill. The inverted siphon tunnels became a pragmatic alternative to bridging deep valleys with an oversaturation of arches. The Yzeron Siphon Bridge (also known as the Beaunant Siphon Bridge) is a prime example of this technique located within a suburb of Lyon.

The majority of the water flow remained underground. Complex piping systems concealed unwarranted access, encroaching neighbors and protected the network against erosion. The troughs were constructed deep and lined with clay to prevent water leakage. Within settlements, the fresh spring water was stored in a concentrated tank called a *castellum*. From this location, smaller pipes branched out into fountains, public baths and for the privileged, directly into their household. Manholes and shafts were constructed to enable access for inspecting and cleaning the subterranean system.

The aqueduct arches were composed of stone, brick and fastened by volcanic cement called *pozzolana* that served as mortar. The strength and durability of the bonding would survive centuries. Temporary wooden scaffolding was constructed to enable elevated access.

Completed Roman aqueducts required decades to complete employing slaves for the brutal and hazardous construction work. Their tasks concentrated on ditch-digging and stone hauling. A water curator supervised the operation, repairs and upgrades. Sluice gates were employed to redirect water away towards an alternative path from damaged pipes.

From Saint-Chamond, the aqueduct flowed northward towards Genilac in the Loire department. The construction swerved abruptly west at the outskirts towards neighboring Chagnon. This path followed the course of the Dureze River.

The route abruptly returned back in the direction of Genilac, bypassing the village, before heading north to the outskirts of Chabaniere. Three significant underground tunnels are incorporated into that routing.

Bypassing Chabaniere, the path continued its circuitous routing until reaching the center of Mornant. The hillsides surrounding the community offer traces of the system's tunneling and canal network. The landscape has altered little over the centuries with remnants of arches still intact. Within the commune of Mornant is a castellum along with various access entrances into the water system.

The aqueduct continued north past the present day communes of St-Laurent d'Agny, Taluyers, Orlienas, Soucieu-en-Jarrest and Brignais before arriving in Chaponost. Each village bares testament to construction traces in the form of decaying arches, siphon bridges and tunneling. The archways of Chaponost overwhelm these modest reminders.

Ninety-two arches situated in the northeastern corner of the village comprise a stretch called *Le Plat de l'Air*. The concentration offers a bold time capsule and intimate glimpse of the construction techniques. The ruins recede organically into countryside of grazing cattle and farmland. The majority of the arches are directly approachable to visitors. The population of Chaponost today hovers towards 9,000 residents.

From the rural spectacle to the approaching metropolis, one final majestic discovery awaits. The tentacles of urban Lyon reveal the Yzeron River Siphon Bridge (also known as Beaunant Siphon Bridge). A meandering village roadway splits two major bridge components accommodating local vehicle traffic. The extended span stretches 2,660 feet between two reservoirs including a drop of 400 feet between the receiving reservoir and the siphon bridge.

The enormity of this exampled engineering feat is magnified by the realization that without the siphon bridges, an enormous elevated structure would be required to carry the water directly into Lugdunum. Such a construction would be unprecedented and likely impossible.

The aqueduct followed the Saint-Foy-Les Lyon plateau in nearly a straight line. That routing alternated between underground tunneling and above ground exposure transported on walls or arches. The path is traced along the present day rue de Narcel and rue George Clemenceau. It continues crossing the Parc du Brulet where portions of the underground channel are visible.

The waters were then directed towards Fourviere Hill within the 5th arrondissement inside the present day Fort Saint-Irenee. The Trion siphon is located inside the grounds of the fortress constructed between 1832 and 1842. The precise location of the aqueduct's terminating reservoir is speculated to be located at the extremity of rue Roger-Radisson. There is no specific marking of the former exact location. Time and human development have covered those tracks.

The enormity and difficulty behind the entire Gier Aqueduct construction process has historically never received the accolades of another iconic Roman bridge located further south. The Pont du Gard, stationed near Remoulins in the Gard department is the most commonly cited and recognized Roman engineering masterpiece.

The monumental scale of the Aqueduct of the Gier is arguably more impressive, particularly considering the capricious and inhospitable terrain required to navigate upon. The Gier aqueduct passed through eleven tunnels, thirty stretches in the open air and ten stretches raised on walls and arches. Most historians agree that it was built as a single concentrated campaign, as no portion could have been operational until it was fully completed.

The Aqueduct of the Gier was one of four created to transport fresh water into Lugdunum. Each employed the penstock process and siphon tunneling to regulate water flow. The second longest was the Aqueduct of the Brevenne that covered 43 miles from the east. The Aqueduct of L'Yzeron crosses 17 miles from the southeast and the Aqueduct of Mount D'Or (Gold Mountain) descends 16 miles from the north.

The term *Traboule* was formally introduced in 1894. These clandestine passageways wind their route through buildings, courtyards and intricate staircases. Each passage is unique and often features buildings with pastel colors, confounding curves, arches, vaulted ceilings and spiral staircases. Each traboule radiates mystery and intrigue within the shadows. Many boast a Renaissance era heritage with some dating back to reportedly the 4th century.

The term traboule is a corruption of the Latin *trans-ambulare* meaning to *pass through*. An estimated 400 traboules exist within Lyon with approximately 40 identified by a small blue lion emblem and open to public access. Inhabitants of the Roman colony of Lugdunum established residences on the banks of the Saone River due to the lack of fresh running water. The lower *Vieux Ville* (old city) settlement was established at the foot of Fourviere Hill. The traboules were designed to permit expedient access for residents to the river.

The Canut silk workers became a prominent presence in the neighborhoods during the early 19th century. They employed the passageways to carry their heavy textile workloads from their Croix-Rousse district workshops to textile merchants at the foot of the hill. The neighborhood became a vortex for union protest sessions to air out complaints to management. Protest often turned violent. There were an estimated 25,000 Canuts living within Lyon. Revolts and protests by the workers often clogged up the neighboring transportation routes. Over 10,000 Canuts were tried in Paris and often faced criminal deportation.

During the World War II Nazi occupation, traboules became excellent clandestine organizing sites for the

French resistance. German soldiers venturing into the darkened space often found themselves within a deathtrap. The maze of passageways was critical for expedient escapes.

Many of the traboules fell into disrepair and neglect during the post-war years. During the 1990s, the city of Lyon agreed to subsidize their restoration in exchange for public visiting privileges. The stated agreed upon hours were between 8 am and 7 pm. Their popularity has resulted in excessive visitation and unwelcome noise outside of those parameters.

Entering the traboule universe often begins with the opening of a wards entrance door that may or may not be accommodating to your discovery quest. Some are locked or require an entrance code. The interior dimly lit corridors often appear foreboding and sinister. Light switches are generally illuminated, but the length of their duration may leave you stranded in darkness if your pace is not sufficiently swift.

Some traboules offer commercial shops and restaurants. Many feature towering multi-levels, staircases and courtyards within the interior. Gated entry passages to subterranean tunnel are habitually locked and prohibited from visitation.

INSIDER SERIES BOOKS.com

1 rue Constantine to 1 quai Pecherie
Lyon 69001

27 rue Saint-Jean to 1 rue des Trois Maries
Lyon 69005

3 rue des Antonins to 68 rue Saint-Jean
69005 Lyon

4 rue Desiree to 7 rue Puits-Gaillot
Lyon 69001

6-8 Petite rue des Feuillants to 19 place Tolozan Lyon 69001

6 rue des Capucins to 1 rue Sainte-Marie-des-Terreaux
Lyon 69001

6 rue Rene-Leynaud to 3-5 rue des Capucins Lyon 69001

7 rue des Capucins
Lyon 69001

Traboule de la Tour Rose
16 rue du Boeuf
Lyon 69005

22 rue des Capucins to 5 rue Coustou
Lyon 69001

33-37 rue August-Comte to 21-25 rue de Remparts-D'Ainay
Lyon 69002

37 place Bellecour to 1 rue du Plat
Lyon 69002

Passage des Imprimeurs
56 rue Merciere to 26 quai St. Antoine
Lyon 69002

Cour Des Voraces
9 place Colbert
Lyon 69001

20 rue Imbert-Colomes to 55 rue des Tables-Claudiennes
Lyon 69001

La Longue Traboule
54 rue Saint-Jean
Lyon 69005

La Maison des Avocats
Place La Bascoche, 60 rue Saint-Jean
Lyon 69005

15 rue Victor-Hugo to 16 rue Auguste Comte
Lyon 69002

Passage Thiaffair
30 rue Burdeau to 19 rue Rene-Leynaud
Lyon 69001

Punaise Passage (Blocked Off)
Lyon

ADDITIONAL TRABOULES:

Lyon 60001
Traboule de Maison Brunet-Canut Revolt, 10 rue Rivet,
Traboule de Maison Brunet-Canut Revolt, 5 place Saint-Catherine
118 Mount of the Grande-Cote to 7 rue Terme
5 rue Royale to 3 quai Lasagne

Lyon 60002
Rue des Trois Passages to 5 place Gailleton
2 rue Charles-Dullin to 1 rue Gaspard-Andre
5 rue Confort to 3 rue David Girin
82 rue President Edouard Herriot to 45 rue de Brest

Lyon 60005
2 place du Gouvernment to 10 quai Romain Rolland
5 rue Juiverie to 3 place Saint-Paul
5 place Neuve Saint-Jean to 40 rue Saint-Jean
2 place du Petit College to 10 rue Saint-Jean

Pedestrian Promenades

Lyon is a pedestrian-friendly city burdened by steep and flinty inclines. The inlaid stone pathways and staircases reveal stunning architecture, commercial offerings and ancient historic sites. Many of the routes were developed amidst some of Lyon's most turbulent and influential events.

Montée Coquillat

Montée de L'Amphiteatre

Montée du Greillon

Montée Rater

Montee St. Bartholemew

Passage Mermet

Passage Colbert

Rue Pouteau

Rue St. Marie des Terreaux

Saone River Bridges

l'le Barbe Bridge (1827)

The I'le Barbe is situated in the middle of the Saone River in the 9th arrondissement. The suspension road bridge was constructed in 1827 replacing a wooden bridge built in 1734. The span is the oldest operating in Lyon connecting to the I'le Barbe (Savage Island). A fifth century abbey was the first monastic establishment in all of Gaul. King Charlemagne established a library that was rumored to contain the *Holly Grail*. The monastery was pillaged and destroyed by marauding tribes including the Saracens and Huns and later Protestant troops. During the French Revolution, remaining items and structures were sold and dispersed.

Pont du General Koenig (1972)

Passerelle de l'Homme-de-la-Roche (1986)

Passerelle Saint Vincent (1832)

Pont La Feuillée (1950)

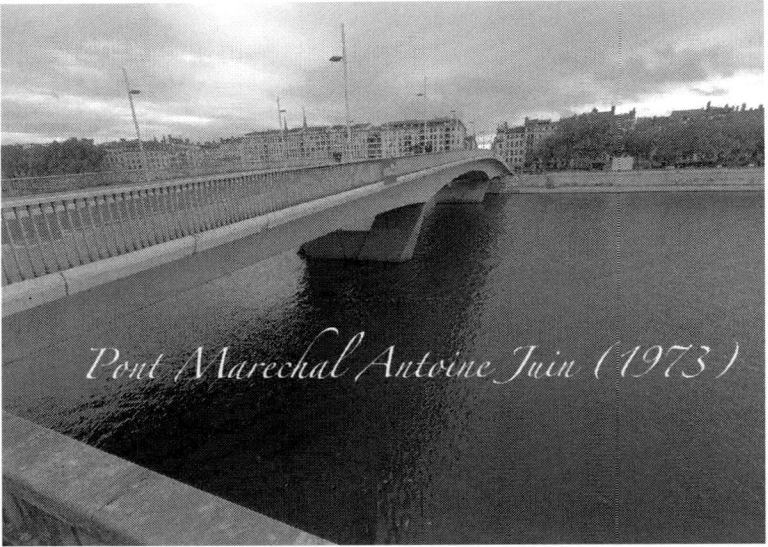

Pont Maréchal Antoine Juin (1973)

Passerelle du Palais du Justice (1983)

Pont Bonaparte (1950)

Passerelle Saint Georges (1944)

Rhone River Bridges

Pont Winston Churchill (1982)

Lattre-de-Tassigny Bridge (1956)

Morand Bridge (1976)

Passerelle du Collège (1845)

Pont Lafayette (1890)

Pont Wilson (1918)

Pont de la Guillotiere (1958)

Pont de l'Universite (1899)

Pont Gallieni (1965)

Author, photographer and visual artist Marques Vickers was born in 1957 in Vallejo, California. He graduated from Azusa Pacific University in Los Angeles and became the Public Relations and Executive Director for the Burbank, California Chamber of Commerce between 1979-84.

Professionally, he has operated travel, apparel, wine, rare book and publishing businesses. His paintings and sculptures have been exhibited in art galleries, private collections and museums in the United States and Europe. He has previously lived in the Burgundy and Languedoc regions of France and currently lives in the South Puget Sound region of Western Washington.

He has written and published over one hundred and thirty books spanning a diverse variety of subjects including true crime, international travel, social satire, wine production, architecture, history, fiction, auctions, fine art, poetry and photojournalism.

He has two daughters, Charline and Caroline who reside in Europe.

Made in the USA
Las Vegas, NV
27 July 2024

93009626R00125